D0001479

Women Work & Worship
—A Study Guide

by Debbie Morgan
With the Women Work & Worship Study Group of
Northlea United Church

Edited by Nancy E. Hardy

Contents
Introduction
Note to Leaders
Sessions
Appendices
Resources

About the author: Debbie Morgan, a student at the Toronto School of Theology, prepared this guide while she served as Pastoral Intern at Northlea United Church in Toronto. A native of St. Catharines and a philosophy graduate from Trent University in Peterborough, Debbie is particularly interested in the area of feminist theology and women's studies in the church. Debbie and Jonathan Morgan live in Toronto with their young son, Jonathan.

THE DIVISION OF

MISSION IN CANADA

Copyright © 1984
The United Church of Canada
All Rights Reserved
ISBN 0-88622-166-8
1st printing 1M 6/84 CS

INTRODUCTION

Last year, I was invited by a UCW unit to speak about women's participation in The United Church of Canada. I gladly agreed, thinking that there would be plenty of material available on the subject. Sadly, I was wrong. There were few such books, and all were limited in their scope. In my search for information, however, I learned about the upcoming publication of a book that might solve my problem: that book was **Women Work & Worship.**

After reading an advance copy, I became convinced that this was an important book for the United Church. It encompassed a broad range of perspectives, looking at the contributions and experiences of a wide range of churchwomen, from traditional to radical. Because of its wide scope, I felt the book needed a study guide if it were to be examined in congregations. Such a guide would have to be written in consultation with a group of churchwomen if it were to be effective. With the support of the Division of Mission in Canada and the commitment of a group of creative and insightful women at Northlea United Church in Toronto, the publication of this study guide was made possible.

This guide evolved from the group's reading, study, and evaluation of the session outlines. Because a number of people were involved in this way, the spirit of co-operation that made **Women Work & Worship** such a special book was also alive in the development of the study guide.

Our study group had many stimulating discussions, as well as much laughter and sharing. It is my hope and the hope of all the members of the Women Work & Worship Study Group that users of this guide will have as much enjoyment in studying the book as we had in developing the guide.

Shalom,

Debbie Morgan, Pastoral Intern,
Northlea United Church, May, 1984

The members of the Northlea Women Work & Worship Study Group were as follows:

Lois Andrews	Norma Crawford	Beth Laing
Loraine Beckley	Jan Fullerton	Ann Loucks
Lola F. Best	Mary Gardhouse	Jacqueline Morris
Jeanne Connell	Patricia Hamilton	Dorothy Saunders

Special thanks to Deborah Marshall of the Division of Mission in Canada for her support and work on the development of this study guide, and to Nancy E. Hardy for editing this guide.

Note to Leaders

This study guide is made up of ten sessions, each approximately one hour long. It is written in such a way that it should need a minimum of leadership responsibility. However, here are some leadership ideas which you may find useful:

1. Read each session a few days before the meeting in case any materials are required (i.e. magic markers, newsprint) or, as in the case of Session Seven, the participants may have to be called and reminded to bring something for the session.

2. If the group is a new one, you may want to use some ice-breakers to open the first session. Have name-tags available and be sure to be on hand to welcome first arrivals. If the members do not know one another, break up into pairs and have one of the pair introduce the other one to the group. Another interesting thing to do is to have each person introduce herself and then tell the group what she was doing last Tuesday (or Thursday or whatever). Interesting revelations will follow! Or go around the circle, have each introduce herself and complete this sentence (or one like it), "I hope this group will...; When I think of women's groups I wish...; Another group I enjoyed being with did..."

3. The sessions are designed so the leaders can read the directions for each question aloud, and the group can then share their answers or do the activity indicated. In our group, if the conversation lagged, or went on too long, the leader would suggest moving on to the next question. The leader also acted as time-keeper.

4. All the sessions suggest closing with prayer. You might want to ask a group member to prepare a closing prayer for the next meeting, or you may wish to write one yourself. A list of worship resources can be found at the end of this guide. We found, however, that prayers written by women in the group were both beautiful and relevant.

5. The most important tip is to relax. In these sessions, all the participants carry some of the responsibility for making the discussions work. The leader is there simply to keep the group on track, and to enter into the discussion herself.

6. The author welcomes feedback on the usefulness of this study guide. Direct comments to Debbie Morgan, Ministry with Adults — Women, c/o Division of Mission in Canada, United Church of Canada, 85 St. Clair Ave. E., Toronto, Ontario, M4T 1M8.

Using the Study Guide

a. Each of the ten-hour-long sessions has been divided into sections: warm-up; Part A; Part B; reflection. If you wish to use this guide for the programme sections of established group meetings, you may want to use a shortened version of each session. For example, you might choose to do only Part A or Part B, or some questions out of both. Use your discretion.

Your group may not wish to spend ten sessions on studying **Women Work & Worship.** While the only way to cover the whole book is to use the ten sessions, it would certainly be worthwhile to pick the sessions which you feel might be most relevant to your group in the time you have. Perhaps you could appoint a small "monitoring group" (of 2 or 3) to keep track of where the group is going, and what seems to interest them most.

b. Another way of using this guide is to form a new study group to use **Women Work & Worship.** We did this at Northlea and found it very enriching. A cross-section of women participated, of varying ages and backgrounds, both UCW and non-UCW women. Because of the diversity of the group, discussions tended to be lively and challenging as well as informative.

c. Don't worry about the number of women in your group. Groups of 10 or fewer members will invite more intimate discussion, while larger groups allow for a wide range of perspective and input. If your group is large, divide into smaller sections of 6-8; be sure to allow time for total group feedback. Our attendance varied from 6-14, but we always found the conversations worthwhile.

SESSION ONE

Purpose: To discuss the formation of churchwomen's groups using our experience today as a guide.
Reading: Chapter 1 — "Women Together — The Call to Collective Action" (pages 5-26)
Warm-up: Discuss any insights gained from the reading. (10 minutes)

Part A

(Use only A *or* B for a short programme; use both parts for a whole meeting devoted to the study.)
1. Chapter 1 points out that women's groups were formed to provide fellowship and cultural and intellectual stimulation for their often isolated members. They also provided an opportunity for women to share their own faith concerns. What are some of the major needs of women in your community? How do they compare with the needs of women in the past? Discuss. (10 minutes)
2. Churchwomen's groups were also formed around the need to meet pressing social concerns. During the Depression, for example, women worked to support needy families, as well as their own churches and mission fields. What are some of the major social problems women in your neighbourhood are most concerned about? (e.g. unemployment, drugs, wife abuse, etc.) How do these compare with the social problems facing our foremothers? Discuss. (10 minutes)
COFFEE BREAK: 10 minutes

Part B

3. Taking into consideration the needs of women in your community and the pressing social concerns facing them, imagine that you are going to form a new churchwomen's group (apart from the UCW structure). What goals would you want that group to have? Discuss. (10 minutes)
4. Together write a statement of purpose for your new group, giving some idea of why the group was formed and what you would like to achieve. Record this 6-8-line statement on a sheet of paper or newsprint. How do you think it compares with the old statement of purpose of the WMS and WA on page 177? What are the differences? Similarities? Discuss. (10 minutes)

Reflection: Each share the strongest insight gained from the discussion on Chapter 1. When it feels appropriate, you may want to close with a prayer or reading.

Preparation for Next Session:
(i) Think about the women's groups you have known and the part money played in those groups.
(ii) Read **Women Work & Worship,** Chapter 2, "Faith and Finances" (pages 27-38).

SESSION TWO

Purpose: To explore the role finances and fund-raising have played in women's work and worship.
Reading: Chapter 2 — "Faith and Finances" (pages 27-38)
Warm-up: Discuss any insights gained from the reading. (10 minutes)

Part A

1. "Faith and Finances" discusses many of the creative methods churchwomen have devised to raise money. Share together some of your most memorable fund-raising efforts. Have you been aware of any changes in fund-raising methods over the past 10 years? If there have been changes, why do you think they have occurred? (10 minutes)
2. "Faith and Finances" points out that fund-raising has been both a justification for the existence of churchwomen's groups as well as a way of achieving the varied objectives of the women gathered together. How do you understand the role of fund-raising and finances in women's groups in your congregation? (e.g. Is fund-raising vital to the existence of the groups?) Is this a change from the role of finances and fund-raising in the churchwomen's groups of the past? How does it compare? (10 minutes)
COFFEE BREAK: 10 minutes

Part B

3. Name some of the things for which women have traditionally raised money. Why have these items been chosen for fund-raising? Discuss. (10 minutes)
4. Imagine that you are a new churchwomen's group (not UCW) and have managed to raise $2,500.00 since your formation a year ago. Speculate how you will use that money. Draw up a budget. Because you are a new church-women's organization, you have no prior guidelines from which to plan. You have the freedom to spend the money as you see fit. Compare your budget with your lists of traditional budget concerns (shown in question 3). How are the lists similar? Different? Why? (10 minutes)

Reflection: Each share one word that best describes how you feel about fund-raising and finances. When appropriate, close with prayer.

Preparation for Next Session:
(i) Think about the term "social change". What does it mean? How does it affect you?
(ii) Read **Women Work & Worship,** Chapter 3, "Social Change Reflected in Women's Work and Worship" (pages 39-62).

SESSION THREE

Purpose: To investigate the ways social change has affected and continues to affect women's work and worship.

Reading: Chapter 3 — "Social Change Reflected in Women's Work and Worship" (pages 39-62)

Warm-up: Share any insights gained from the reading. (10 minutes)

Part A

1. With what social change/concern/movement described in chapter 3 did you most identify? Why? Have you been committed to a particular movement in the past 10 years? What has it been? What has that commitment involved in terms of work, time, effect on family life and/or relationships? (10 minutes)

2. For churchwomen of the past, their activities in social movements were part and parcel of their faith commitment. What role has your faith and church life played in your commitment to social concerns? (10 minutes)

COFFEE BREAK: 10 minutes

Part B

3. Read the case study and article in Appendix A and discuss questions which follow:

Case Study You live in a city of 60,000 known as Yourtown. Although Yourtown reflects the national average of two women in ten battered, it has few homes for battered women. All such homes are in the downtown core, since the city has bylaws against group homes in residential areas. A few weeks ago, a local women's group opened a battered women's shelter on a quiet suburban street. It was filled immediately. It was also quickly closed by the local authorities, because of the bylaws. The women's collective which founded the home has approached the women of your church seeking their support in advocating the re-opening of the home. They argue that homes for battered women need to be placed in residential areas where the women will feel less isolated, and where their children can go to school and live in a calm environment, away from the downtown core where the bylaws are not as restrictive. They say that the reason they opened the home in the suburbs despite the bylaw, was because the city council had repeatedly chosen to ignore the issue.

Questions: (20 minutes)

a) Discuss the case study and the article in Appendix A. Would you as a group support the shelter, and if necessary, present your stand to the committees and groups in your congregation? Why? Have any situations like this arisen in your neighbourhood/district? How has your church reacted?

b) If you could agree to support the shelter, what are some of the ways you could advocate/support them?

Note: In both questions, how can you link your decision to your faith and/or biblical witness?

Reflection: Consider the work of our foremothers at the head of such social

3

movements as temperance and pacifism. What roles do you think church-women's organizations should play with regard to social concerns in the future? When appropriate, close with prayer.

Preparation for Next Session:
(i) Think about the relationship between your women's group and the national church. Has it been a happy one? Could it do with some changing?
(ii) Read **Women Work & Worship,** Chapter 4, "The Past as a Guide to the Future" (pages 63-82).

SESSION FOUR

Purpose: To examine the relationship between churchwomen's groups and the institutional church and pose some questions about the future.
Reading: Chapter 4 — "The Past as a Guide to the Future" (pages 63-82)
Warm-up: Share any insights gained in the reading. (10 minutes)

Part A

1. In Chapter 4, **Women Work & Worship** invites us to talk about the changing nature of women's groups in the United Church, particularly the UCW.
If you are a member of the UCW, how did you feel about Shirley Davy's percep-tions? In your view, are they accurate, inaccurate or somewhere in the middle? What are some of the things, if any, you'd like to change about the UCW struc-ture (e.g. look particularly at the section about pyramids and circles, page 70) and/or its relationship with the church? Discuss. (20 minutes)
COFFEE BREAK: 10 minutes

Part B

2. Shirley Davy is committed to a social change which is rooted in and learns from the radical commitments of our foremothers. From your reading of **Women Work & Worship** and your own experience, what elements of women's ministries and group formation would you like to incorporate into women's groups in the church today? Why? (10 minutes)
3. Shirley Davy lists integration, project-oriented groups, and special interest groups as possible directions for women's groups to go in the future. How do you react to her suggestions? What form do you see churchwomen's groups taking in the near and/or distant future? What relationship might they have to the whole church (on the congregational, presbyterial and national level)? (10 minutes)

Reflection: Each take a sheet of paper and a pencil and draw a symbol each per-son feels best reflects the changes taking place with churchwomen's groups.

4

Share symbols and what they represent. When appropriate, close in prayer.

Preparation for Next Session:
(i) Think about women ministers you know or have known.
(ii) Read *Women Work & Worship,* Chapter 5, "A Lady in the Pulpit" (pages 83-105).

SESSION FIVE

Purpose: To examine the ways women have approached professional ministry within The United Church of Canada and the way the church has responded to those ministries.

Reading: Chapter 5 — "A Lady in the Pulpit" (pages 83-105)

Warm-up: Share any insights gained in the reading. (10 minutes)

Part A

Two streams of professional ministry recognized by The United Church of Canada are the diaconal and ordained ministries. Although this definition is by no means definitive, the diaconal ministry tends to be concerned with Christian education and has had a strong emphasis on the empowerment of lay people at all levels of the church. The ordained ministry has most frequently had a focus on worship and sacraments, and on pastoral oversight. However, these aspects are not exclusive to one group only. Frequently, a diaconal person will be in worship leadership; as well, many ordained ministers see education as an important aspect of their work. At present, women form four percent of the ordained ministry and ninety-three percent of the diaconal ministry.

1. Appendix B lists some quotes from women in diaconal or ordained ministry, sharing their sense of call. Have you experienced some sense of Christian calling? When? What was it like? Share your experience with the group. (15 minutes)

2. Women in professional ministry experience differing receptions from their congregations. For many, recognition of women as equal to men in the pulpit did not come easily. What problems do you think an ordained woman might encounter in your congregation? A diaconal woman? List. Look at Appendix C which lists comments by different women about how they were received. How do they compare with your list? Discuss. (15 minutes)

COFFEE BREAK: 10 minutes

Part B

3. Have you had a female minister either as permanent staff or visiting preacher? Or visited a church whose minister was a woman? What was your reaction (thoughts, emotions, etc.)? Why do you feel you reacted as you did? Discuss. (15 minutes)

4. As women become more and more visible in professional ministry, how do

5

you feel the church as a whole will be affected? Discuss. (10 minutes)

Reflection: Each share the one female biblical figure whom you feel best represents what ministry is all about. Share why you chose your figure. When appropriate, you may want to close in prayer.

Preparation for Next Session:
(i) Think about the term "ministry". Where do you fit in?
(ii) Read **Women Work & Worship,** Chapter 6, "Ministering to One Another" (pages 106-129).

SESSION SIX

Purpose: To examine the ways women have approached ministry in the church, and the way the church has responded to and understood women's ministries.

Reading: Chapter 6 — "Ministering to One Another" (pages 106-129)

Warm-up: Share any insights gained in the reading. (10 minutes)

Part A

1. The *Concise Oxford Dictionary* defines the term "minister" as one who renders aid or service. It also speaks of the clergy as ministers. On a sheet of paper, have each person draw an image (picture, symbol, cartoon, etc.) that the word "ministry" brings forth. Have the pictures shared and explained. (15 minutes)

2. Share your memories of the women in your life that you most admired and respected. What inspired you about those women? (15 minutes)

COFFEE BREAK: 10 minutes

Part B

3. As our own stories show, our foremothers brought many gifts with them to Christian ministry. What are the gifts or talents you bring to ministry? Where and how do you apply them? (15 minutes)

4. We have discussed the many ministries of women in the United Church. How has the church understood these ministries? How do you account for those understandings? (10 minutes)

Reflection: Share in the reading of the litany on ministry on page 158 of **Women Work & Worship.** Does it express the way you feel about ministry? When appropriate, you may want to close in prayer.

Preparation for Next Session:
(i) Think about the experiences that have shaped your faith and your life in the church.

(ii) Read **Women Work & Worship,** Chapter 7, "Women, Work and Worship" (pages 131-164).
(iii) Bring a personal "patchwork piece" to the next meeting. This can be anything that reflects a memorable aspect or experience of your church or faith life.

SESSION SEVEN

Purpose: To share the "patchwork pieces" or our experience in the church and assess their effect on our lives.
Reading: Chapter 7 — **"Women Work and Worship"** (pages 131-164).
Preparation: Each bring a personal "patchwork piece" to the meeting. These may be any objects which reflect a memorable aspect/experience of your church or faith life.
Warm-up: Each share any insights gained in the reading. (10 minutes)

Part A

1. Share your patchwork pieces and the experiences they symbolize. If yours is a large group, divide into smaller sections so each person can have a chance to share what she has brought. (20 minutes)
2. Our lives are made up of patchwork pieces — experiences that make us who we are. What religious or church experiences have been formative for you? Share. In groups of three or more, write a poem or create a symbol which reflects your experience as women in the church. (15-20 minutes)
COFFEE BREAK: 10 minutes

Part B

3. In the larger group, share your poems and/or symbols. (10 minutes)
4. If a piece is missing, or badly sewn, a quilt's appearance may be greatly altered. How might your life be different, had you not had those experiences which you shared? Reflect and share. (10 minutes)

Reflection: There are many kinds of patchwork quilts: log cabin, wedding ring, rose wreath, patchwork, morning-glory, postage stamp, crazy quilts, courthouse square, tulip, oak leaf, and many others. Ask each person to choose a quilt name which best reflects the combination of her personal experiences in the church. When appropriate, close in prayer. (15 minutes)

Preparation for Next Session:
(i) Think about the term "power". Where does power lie within The United Church of Canada?
(ii) Read **Women Work & Worship,** Chapter 8, "Women and Power in The United Church of Canada" (pages 170-188) and Chapter 9, "Christian Feminism in the United Church: Resources in Culture and Tradition" (pages 189-205).

SESSION EIGHT

Purpose: To explore our understandings of Christian feminism and how we experience "power" within the United Church.
Reading: Chapter 8 — "Women and Power in The United Church of Canada" (pages 170-188); Chapter 9 — "Christian Feminism in the United Church: Resources in Culture and Tradition" (pages 189-205)
Warm-up: Discuss any insights gained from the reading. (10 minutes)

Part A

1. In pages 173-174, Shelagh Parsons touches on some of the historical bases of sexism, and affirms some of the hidden details of women's "herstory." What information did you find surprising? Not surprising? Why? (10 minutes)
2. Shelagh Parsons points out that the amalgamation of the WMS and WA meant a loss of the economic power formerly held by the WMS. The women exchanged this for the possibility of greater integration of women into all aspects of church life. Do you think women gained enough to warrant the sacrifice of their financial power and influence? If the WMS were in existence today, and you were members, would you consider amalgamation with the WA? If so, what issues would you take into consideration? What would you want in exchange for your economic influence? If you would not amalgamate, share reasons for your decision. (15 minutes)

COFFEE BREAK: 10 minutes

Part B

3. The word "power" has both negative and positive implications. It can mean "power over", where control and resources rest in the hands of a privileged few and access to power is granted by the minority rather than being the right of all persons. It can also mean "empowerment", where every individual has equal and direct access to resources, as well as control over their own lives. Empowerment encourages a sense of affirmation and self-worth. When have you experienced either kind of power in any aspect of church life? In what church committees/organizations have you felt most empowered? Disempowered? What particular experiences brought those feelings forward? Share your experiences. (20 minutes)
4. Chapter 9 discusses various understandings of Christian feminism. Define what the term "Christian feminism" means to you. What biblical passages or persons might be important to an understanding of Christian feminism? What specific concerns might be part of its focus? Have you seen Christian feminism reflected in the life of your congregation and/or personal faith journey? Do you consider yourself a Christian feminist or in sympathy with some of the concerns and beliefs of Christian feminism? Why? (20 minutes)

Reflection: Word association. Each person share one word that comes to mind

8

when the word "woman" is said. Then stand, holding hands and have someone in the group lead in a closing prayer. (10 minutes)

Preparation for Next Session:
(i) Think about the language used in the church. Is it inclusive (includes both men and women in its terminology) or is it dominated by male terms and male imagery?
(ii) Read *Women Work & Worship,* Chapter 10, "Side Road on the Journey to Autonomy: The Diaconate Prior to Church Union" (pages 206-227), and Chapter 11, "Liberating Christianity" (pages 228-235).

SESSION NINE

Purpose: To examine our experience in liberating images of our faith, and in that light look back at how women functioned in the diaconate before church union.
Readings: Chapter 10 — "Side Road on the Journey to Autonomy: The Diaconate Prior to Church Union" (pages 206-227); Chapter 11 — "Liberating Christianity" (pages 228-235).
Warm-up: Share any insights you gained from the readings. (10 minutes)

Part A

1. Chapter 11 speaks of Christianity as liberating. In what ways could Christ be perceived as a liberator? What makes the Bible a liberating book for you? An oppressive book? (10-15 minutes)

2. Margie Whynot speaks of the language of faith. How do you feel about such language as "pagan", "heathen", "girls" (when referring to adult women), "sons of God", "mankind", "Heavenly Father"? Do you experience them as "inclusive"? "exclusive"? Printed below are two versions of the same hymn. Do you prefer one version to another, or are both equally acceptable to you? Share your preference, and reasons behind them.

His sovereign power
without our aid
Made us of clay
and formed us men;
And when like
wandering sheep
we strayed
He brought us to
his fold again. (Isaac Watts)

God's sovereign power
without our aid
Formed and created us
of clay;
And when like
wandering sheep
we strayed
God brought us back
into the way.

What images or language describing God have been the most meaningful in your faith life?

Have one of the women read aloud the story in Appendix D. How do you res-

9

pond to the story? Could such an incident happen in your church? With whom do you identify — the mother or daughter? (15-20 minutes for Question 2.) COFFEE BREAK: 10 minutes

Part B

3. What do you perceive were the most liberating aspects of the diaconal vocation? The most oppressive? Do you agree with Diane Haglund's comments at the end of the chapter: "In women's long journey toward autonomy in the church, the diaconate represents a side road. The office says much about women's relationship to mainline Protestantism, but ultimately it represents a dead-end" (page 227)? Why or why not? (15 minutes)

4. In many ways, the diaconate symbolized the contrasting experiences of women committed to church vocations at the turn of the century. On the one hand, it epitomized the vision of the Social Gospel movement — caring for the poor, visiting the ill. On the other hand, its demands were so onerous that the diaconate became known as "holy drudgery". It offered women a new religious role that was accepted and supported by the institutional church. Yet in doing so, it was a trade-off in an era when the major denominations were affirming the non-ordination of women and the exclusion of women from the courts of the church.

If you were a middle-class woman in the era before church union, would you have considered the diaconate as a possible vocation? Why? If not, which of the following acceptable careers of women might you have chosen, and why? Homemaker; nurse; social worker; tract society organizer; missionary (as doctor, nurse, evangelist); teacher; temperance activist; secretary; sales clerk. If none of these possibilities appeal to you, might you have chosen the route of the radical activists, such as Sarah Grimke and Nellie McClung? Why? (15-20 minutes)

Reflection: Share the religious symbol (i.e. cross, dove, chalice, etc.) that you feel best reflects the liberating power of the Christian faith for you. When appropriate, you may want to close in prayer. (10 minutes)

Preparation for Next Session:
(i) Think about memorable women within the church. What were they like? What can they teach us?
(ii) Read **Women Work & Worship,** Chapter 12, "Pouring the Tea and Hiding The Wine Bottle" (pages 236-248), and Chapter 13, "The Influence of Ruth Tillman on Women in Ministry" (pages 249-260).

SESSION TEN

Purpose: (a) To explore the influence of certain memorable women in our lives, such as women married to ministers, individuals such as Ruth Tillman, and our own influence on the lives of others.

(b) To examine our expectations and perceptions of ministers' spouses and how those perspectives have influenced their role in the church.

(c) To reflect on the experiences of this study time together.

Readings: Chapter 12 — "Pouring the Tea and Hiding the Wine Bottle: Reflections on the Role of the Minister's Mate" (pages 236-248); Chapter 13 — "The Influence of Ruth Tillman on Women in Ministry" (pages 249-260).

Warm-up: Share any insights gained in the reading. (10 minutes)

Part A

1. Chapter 12 discusses the often challenging position of people married to ministers. What influence did the minister's wife have on you and/or your family when you were growing up? What function(s) did she carry in your church community in those years?

What expectations have you had about the role of the minister's spouse in church life? Have your expectations changed over the years? How? How might your expectations have been different if the minister's spouse had been male? How do you feel ministers' spouses experience the expectations of the church community? (i.e. with joy, anger, etc.) Why? (15-20 minutes)

2. Chapter 12 notes that the church work of many ministers' wives are taken for granted... "unordained but usable" ...and at the same time, invisible. Have you yourself experienced the sense that your work is not valued by others, but perceived as invisible — less important than the work of your spouse or family? If so, how have you dealt with that? Share. (10 minutes)

COFFEE BREAK: 10 minutes

Part B

3. Chapter 13 talks of the many girls' groups and camps in which Ruth Tillman worked.

Of what special group or camp were you a part? Share some of your memories of those groups. (15 minutes)

4. Chapter 13 discusses the influence of Ruth Tillman on various women's lives. From your reading, what did you feel were Ruth's most important gifts? All of us, like Ruth, have not lived in isolation — we've touched the life of someone else. What one non-family member have you influenced most? Who has had the most profound influence on your choice of vocation? (15 minutes)

Reflection: Share the most memorable experience you've had in this or any of the Women Work & Worship meetings. When appropriate, you may want to close with the following worship, or a worship time you've prepared yourselves. Feel free to change the worship in any way you feel appropriate.

Worship

Prayer: Gracious, loving God, bless us as we share in worship this evening (morning, afternoon). We place before you our experience as women who have laughed, shared, and grieved together. Support in us a renewed sense of faith, hope, and courage that we will continue to build life-giving bonds of love and commitment for one another, and for all people. Amen.

Scripture Reading: Ephesians 2: 13-19.

Meditation, Poem: (Either written by a group member or taken from one of the resources listed at the end of this guide)

Song/Hymn

Communal Benediction: Starting with the leader, each woman turn to the woman on her left and say: "You are chosen and loved by God, and I am glad."

APPENDIX A

YOURTOWN GAZETTE

CITY HALL DIVIDED OVER WOMEN'S SHELTER City Council was split today over whether the recently closed battered women's shelter on Greenwood Place would be allowed to re-open. Council member R. Hill said in an interview this afternoon, "If we make exceptions for a home for battered women, we have to make exceptions for everyone." When asked for his opinion on Councillor Hill's remarks, Council member Shephard countered that "perhaps that wouldn't be a bad idea, given the need for group homes for the handicapped, and people like those who have been released from mental health institutions." Shephard also noted that the downtown area, not restricted by the bylaw, cut group-home members off from the mainstream of the community. "Both members of the community and group-home members suffer when we do that," he noted. No decision was reached today, and it is expected the discussion will continue in a week's time, after the annual council recess.

APPENDIX B

One of the questions asked of women ministers in the research used in the recently released report on women in ministry was: "Why choose a church vocation?" Over one-third of the women indicated that they felt "the call" to ministry. These are some of their comments describing how they experienced that call: "I first experienced it when I was sixteen, but I ignored it, because I did not think I as a woman would be able to enter the ministry. It happened again when I was 23 and this time I answered."

"I remember having some frank discussion in prayer with God and saying — Are you sure you want me to do this? The answer came back — Yes."

"When I realized that aside from feeling 'right' in this work, that it could be done as a (female) minister rather than just a spouse of a minister."

"A sudden realization that women could be ministers and that God wanted me — feeling of great gratitude and joy towards God."

"At age 16 when my father was suddenly killed in a car accident, and I experienced the presence of God in my bereavement."

"It started as a dream. Frightened to tell anyone, I nursed the idea for years, until I realized it was a call I could not deny. Once I made my goal known, the opportunities opened up. I was happiest in the church. I realized my talent."

From Chapter 2, "Women in Ministry" Report
By: Janet Silman

Commissioned by: Women in Ministry Overview Group, Division of Ministry Personnel and Education, The United Church of Canada.

Used by permission.

APPENDIX C

Those in the women in ministry report who were the first woman to serve in their present position (75% of respondents) were asked if they were aware of any reactions or implications related to their being the first woman. "After initial resistance, ministry accepted" was reported by 30%; 15% reported a favourable reception; 10% felt they were perceived as being on trial; 10% felt trivialized as women — i.e. not taken seriously; 10% experienced open rejection. These are some of their comments:

"Yes, *some* people thought a woman minister was scraping the bottom of the barrel or did not think a woman should be ordained."

"Woman is weaker sex, probably can't cope with northern winters. Men and women worried about me in a 'smothering' way."

"A fuss in the congregation when the pastoral relations committee recommended a woman minister — one elderly man who is solidly with us now stayed away for a month because they didn't choose a male."

"Being a woman minister immediately liberates you from most of the stereotyped expectations of clergy. This has been extremely positive."

"Some people would not come to church — others not sure if I could handle the work — lots of comments at first, 'Well we don't expect you to do what a man would do'."

"Had a few people indicate they wanted a 'real' minister for weddings, funerals. Once people got to know you as a person these reactions disappeared. Some women especially felt they could relate better to a woman minister."

"Not only was I female, I was 40 years younger than the man before me. The church was really down, so they were willing to give me a chance. (A man would not need the 'chance'.) Things really have gone well, if they didn't I'm not sure where I would be."

"There were some assumptions that I could fulfill the role of both minister and minister's wife."

"Recently I was told that some thought I would never last two months."

From Chapter 7, "Women in Ministry" Report.
Used by permission.

14

APPENDIX D

A Mother's Day Story

I want to share a Mother's Day story.

It's about my mother, an independent but traditional woman who has a difficult time understanding her daughter and where my faith journey is taking me.

Mother is a member of a small fundamentalist Baptist church in Massachusetts, in which men do the talking, the praying in mixed company, the serving of the Lord's Supper, and the serious decision-making. The minister is young, male, serious, and treats women solicitously. But he does listen to my mother. *She* keeps the minutes of the church as clerk.

In March I spent a weekend with Mother and attended Sunday school, morning, and evening services with her. At the evening service the song leader announced the hymn, "Faith of Our Fathers". I sang lustily, at least part of the time, "Faith of Our Mothers", and looked carefully at the words. Mother took note but said nothing.

Later that evening, I said, "Mother, do you think the pastor would consider having the congregation sing "Faith of Our Mothers" on Mother's Day this year? I think it would be nice to acknowledge that women as well as men are imprisoned for the gospel and suffer for the faith. What do you think?"

Mother thought a minute and then answered, "Yes, I don't see anything biblically wrong with that. I'll wait until a few weeks after you've gone and then I'll suggest it to the pastor."
Mother did just that.

A few weeks ago, during our ritual Thursday morning phone conversations, she let me know what was happening. "Deborah, I went to the pastor and suggested the change in the wording of "Faith of Our Fathers" — for Mother's Day. He didn't seem to have a problem with it; but he asked that I talk to the song leader and clear it with him. He says fine; he'll have the mixed quartet sing it at the morning service." There were a few more hitches and misunderstandings but mother stuck by her resolve and convinced both men that the change in wording was biblically sound.

Monday morning this week I got the report. Yes, the quartet had sung "Faith of Our Mothers". No one had commented. But mother had felt, well, almost tearful as she heard the new words to the old familiar hymn. She felt, she said, included; she felt important; she felt reborn; she felt like Mother's Day. She has begun to turn her world upside-down.

Deborah Marshall

RESOURCES

Unless otherwise indicated, the following books and resources are available from any CANEC branch. If they are not available from the branch nearest you, ask the CANEC manager to order them for you.

Women's Resources (General)

Biblical Affirmations of Women, Leonard Swidler. Philadelphia: The Westminster Press, 1979 — $12.95.

Our Ministry, Our Lives, Rita Chamberlain and Shelley Finson. Toronto: The United Church of Canada (Division of Mission in Canada), 1981 — $7.80.

Women's Concerns Newsletter — published four times a year by the Ministry with Adults — Women of The United Church of Canada. Order from 85 St. Clair Ave. E., Toronto, ON M4T 1M8 — free.

Women in Ministry Report, Janet Silman. Toronto: The United Church of Canada, 1983. Order from the Division of Ministry Personnel and Education, 85 St. Clair Ave. E., Toronto, ON M4T 1M8 — $2.00.

Women Work & Worship, Shirley Davy. Toronto: The United Church of Canada (Division of Mission in Canada), 1983 — $9.75.

Inclusive Language Resources

An Inclusive Language Lectionary: Readings for Year A. Philadelphia: The Westminster Press, 1983 — $10.75.

Guidelines for Inclusive Language. Toronto: The United Church of Canada (Division of Mission in Canada), 1981 — $1.50.

Worship Resources

Because We Are One People — Songs for Worship. Chicago: Ecumenical Women's Centre, 1978 — $4.95.

Gathering — a packet for worship planners. Published 3 times a year. Toronto: The United Church of Canada (Division of Mission in Canada). Available by subscription from CANEC, 85 St. Clair Ave. E., Toronto, ON M4T 1M8. $10.00 per year.

Images - Women in Transition, Janice Grana, compiler. Nashville: The Upper Room, 1976 — $6.75.

Jesus Christ, Life of the World — A Worship Book from the Sixth Assembly of the World Council of Churches. Geneva: World Council of Churches, 1984 — $8.50.

No Longer Strangers, Iben Gjerding and Katherine Kinnmon, eds. Geneva: The World Council of Churches, 1983 — $5.75.

Seasons of Women, Penelope Washburn, ed. San Francisco: Harper & Row, 1982 — $6.95.

Sisters and Brothers Sing! Sharon and Tom Neufer Emswiler. Normal, Illinois: The Wesley Foundation Campus Ministry, 1977 — $5.95.

16